The Bo

For All Housenoias

OR

THE ART OF PRESERVING ANIMAL AND VEGETABLE SUBSTANCES FOR MANY YEARS

Translated by

K. G. BITTING, M.S.,

Bacteriologist, Glass Container Association

of America.

British Library Cataloguing-in-Publication Data
A catalogue record for this book is available from the
British Library

Preserving and Canning Food: Jams, Jellies and Pickles

Food preservation has permeated every culture, at nearly every moment in history. To survive in an often hostile and confusing world, ancient man was forced to harness nature. In cold climates he froze foods on the ice, and in tropical areas, he dried them in the sun. Today, methods of preserving food commonly involve preventing the growth of bacteria, fungi (such as yeasts), and other micro-organisms, as well as retarding the oxidation of fats that cause rancidity. Many processes designed to conserve food will involve a number of different food preservation methods. Preserving fruit by turning it into jam, for example, involves boiling (to reduce the fruit's moisture content and to kill bacteria, yeasts, etc.), sugaring (to prevent their re-growth) and sealing within an airtight jar (to prevent recontamination). Preservation with the use of either honey or sugar was well known to the earliest cultures, and in ancient Greece, fruits kept in honey were common fare. Quince, mixed with honey, semi-dried and then packed tightly into jars was a particular speciality. This method was taken, and improved upon by the Romans, who *cooked* the quince and honey - producing a solidified texture which kept for much longer. These techniques have remained popular into the modern age, and especially during the high-tide of imperialism, when trading between Europe, India and the Orient was at its peak. This fervour for trade had two fold consequences; the need to preserve a variety of foods - hence we see more 'pickling', and the arrival of sugar cane in Europe. Preserving fruits, i.e. making jams and jellies became especially popular in Northern European countries, as without enough natural sunlight to dry food, this was a fail safe method to increase longevity. Jellies were actually most commonly used for savoury items; some foods, such as eels, naturally form a protein gel when cooked - and this dish became especially popular in the East End of London, where they were (and are) eaten with mashed potatoes. Pickling; the technique of preserving foods in vinegar (or other anti-microbial substances such as brine, alcohol or vegetable oil) also has a long history, again gaining precedence with the Romans, who made a concentrated fish pickle sauce called 'garum'. 'Ketchup' was originally an oriental fish brine which travelled the spice route to Europe (some time during the sixteenth century), and eventually to America, where sugar was finally added to it. The increase in trade with the sub-continent also meant that spices became a common-place item in European kitchens, and they were widely used in pickles to create new and exciting recipes. Soon chutneys, relishes, piccalillis, mustards, and ketchups were routine condiments. Amusingly, Worcester sauce was discovered from a forgotten barrel of special relish in the basement of the Lea and Perrins Chemist shop! As is evident, the story of food preservation, and specifically the modern usages of jams, jellies and pickles encompasses far more than just culinary history. Ancient civilisations, nineteenth century colonialism and accidental discoveries all played a part in creating this staple of our modern diet.

Preserving and Canning Food: Meat Curing

Food preservation has permeated every culture, at nearly every moment in history. To survive in an often hostile and confusing world, ancient man was forced to harness nature. In cold climates he froze foods on the ice, and in tropical areas, he dried them in the sun. Today, methods of preserving food commonly involve preventing the growth of bacteria, fungi (such as yeasts), and other micro-organisms, as well as retarding the oxidation of fats that cause rancidity. The earliest curing consisted of nothing more than dehydration; early cultures utilised salt to help dessicate foods, and this was a well-known technique almost everywhere on the globe. Food curing dates back to ancient times, both in the form of smoked meat and as salt-cured meat. The Plains Indians hung their meat at the top of their teepees to increase the amount of smoke and air coming into contact with the food. Drying, essentially reduces the water content sufficiently to prevent bacterial growth, and salt (or sometimes sugar can be used) draws the moisture from the meat via a process of osmosis. In the 1800s, and before, chefs and lay-people alike experimented with different sources of salt (rock salt, sea salt, spiced salt etc.) and it was discovered that certain types of salt gave meat a red colour, instead of the usual, and somewhat unappetising grey. The active ingredients in this type of salt would have been either nitrates or nitrites, and they also helped inhibit the growth of

Clostridium botulinum; a toxic bacteria often found in old meats. In the new age of consumerism, this technique was soon picked up by butchers and store-keepers alike to appeal an increasingly prosperous population. This salt, often coloured pink to differentiate it from table salt, is now used in cured meat production on a massive scale. Sea salt added to raw ham to make Prosciutto, has became one of the best known, and most expensive exports of central and northern Italy. Today, we do not simply cure and preserve out of necessity, but because we enjoy it.

The art of Appertizing, or preserving food sterilized by heat in a hermetically sealed container, was conceived a little more than a hundred years ago as a war measure to provision the French forces upon the sea. It played a most important part in provisioning the armies in the recent war and in providing succor for the millions of starving civilians. But this role is far less beneficent than is the furnishing of good, wholesome, palatable, nutritious food at all times and at any place under peace conditions.

The food preserving industry has grown with remarkable rapidity in this country during the past two decades, and this applies to the household as well as to the factory or commercial product. As a result, many persons are taking more than a cursory interest in the preparation of their foods, and to some of these a translation of the original work by M. Appert may prove of interest.

The translation has been made to follow the original very closely in order to preserve the exact meaning intended and not to modernize it according to present usage.

NICOLAS APPERT.

Like many inventors and scientists, Nicolas Appert did not reap the benefits from the discoveries which he made on methods of preserving foods, nor did he receive adequate honors, though it was realized by the government even during his lifetime how far-reaching were his discoveries.

M. Appert was born at Chalons-sur-Marne in 1750, and experimented with foods all the working years of his life, as he conducted and superintended the work in confectionaries, kitchens, distilleries, breweries, and store-houses for food, besides being the provisioner to the ducal house of Christian IV., a position which carried assurance that its possessor was of large experience, of executive ability, and of wide knowledge. His experience gave him a thorough and varied knowledge of the preparation of foods, evidenced in his methods for their preservation which show an insight into their structure which is rarely held even by the food manufacturer of today.

Not only does he rank as the originator of the preservation of foods through sterilization by heat in closed vessels, but as a man of generous character, sharing his discoveries with all who wished to use them. He was a man of wide vision, knowing full well the importance to the whole world of the success of his experiments. On the other hand he was very particular to the minutest detail, so that as a result, a tyro, by following his directions, could use his methods successfully. When it is realized that he was obliged to make all the apparatus and appliances which he used, even to designing special bottles, to the making of the corks, cutting and gluing them by hand, the difficulties which he had to meet and overcome seem insurmountable.

The Society for the Encouragement of National Industry drew attention through their official bulletin to the importance of his work, according him much honor. This organization had his work verified under severe conditions by the Bureau of Arts and Manufactures. The foods were carried on voyages, some of these being beyond the equator, and on the boats they were stored under unfavorable conditions. Their importance in eliminating scurvy from seafaring men and in furnishing provisions for the soldiers was realized by ·the French government, and, upon the request of the Minister of the Interior, the detailed description of his work was published, for which he was awarded 12,000 francs as a "testimonial of the good will of the government." His work was published in 1810, though he had a testimonial from the society in April, 1809. and he had been studying and experimenting for ten years previously along these same lines.

Napoleon and his ministers were greatly interested in the development of the sugar beet industry at that time and extended to it unlimited government aid, but evidently through preoccupation with that interest failed to fully recognize the great service which Appert had rendered or to give the full measure of encouragement to him which was his due.

The award furnished him with funds with which to establish his work on a commercial basis, and in 1812 he founded the House of Appert, and remained at the head nearly to the time of his death in 1841. He died a poor man, having exhausted his means in continuing his experiments and in trying to bring them to a higher state of perfection.

He has had worthy successors in members of his family; his immediate successor, M. Raymond Chevallier-Appert, was knighted for the services which he and his family rendered to humanity. He it was who adapted the autoclave to the use of processing foods at temperatures above the boiling point and who also devised a manometer for it so as to regulate the pressure more closely.

and was thus enabled to obtain temperatures varying not more than a half of a
degree. Previously, temperatures
might vary twenty degrees. It was during his ownership that the factory was
moved to the site that it now occupies,
and the name of the manufactory
changed to that of "House of Chevallier-Appert." He was succeeded by
M. Alfred Chevallier-Appert, another
notable member of the family, who in-
stalled additional works, storehouses,
and offices for the various needs of the
work. He received the Cross of Chev-
alier of the Legion of Honor in 1896 for
services rendered the industry. He died
in 1909, after forty years' service, and
was succeeded by his son, Raymond
Chevallier-Appert, second, who did notable work during the war in carrying on
the family tradition for providing wholesome, appetizing food for the soldiers.
He also received the Cross of the Legion
of Honor for his initiative and services.
Associated with Raymond Chevallier-
Appert are many devoted fellow-work-

ers, many of whom have been decorated with the medal of Honor, a recognition made by the government for thirty years' service with the same house.

In the preservation of food Nicolas Appert, not only used a varied assortment, as can be seen from the table of contents, but also prepared them in an appetizing way, not being satisfied to merely preserve the basic material. He also preserved them in forms that are considered achievements in the art of preserving today. In 1814, he requested tests be made of his bouillon cubes. This originality and initiative have been characteristic of the Appert manufactory from the start, and has been carried on through more than the hundred years of its existence. Among its products today are found hors-d'oeuvres, soups, meats *au naturel* and with various dressings, patés, game and domestic fowl, vegetables also prepared in the form of various dishes or *au naturel,* termed *a l'anglaise,* sauces, fish, eggs, cheese, entremets, desserts, fruits, and beverages, so that a catalogue of the products looks like an extensive high class menu, the preparation of which requires not only great skill, but also scientific knowledge of a high order.

While Appert's training was in the school of experience, he was a true scientist. He had the ability to develop facts through carefully planned experiments and to interpret the results in the relation of cause to effect. He set about the task of studying food preservation systematically. No "fortunate accident" served to give him a starting point from which he could proceed with ease. His was the task of blazing a new path through the unknown and this he accomplished by short steps, always going forward and with confidence because that which he had covered was well done. His achievement of success was the result of clear thinking and almost limitless patience in attacking a difficult problem, but which, due to his establishing the correct fundamental principles, seems so simple to us. He is deserving of special honor, for science at that period offered him little or no aid. Bacteriology, the special branch of science upon which his work depends, was then unknown, and chemistry afforded him little assistance. In fact he had a far better understanding of what he was doing than did Gay-Lussac, then the foremost chemist of the world, or Liebig who followed later, both of whom undertook to explain why his products kept.

In many ways Appert deserves to stand in the same relation to the food preserving industry as does Pasteur to the sciences of bacteriology and of medicine. Through his efforts mankind has been benefited by better foods, the surplus product of one season may be safely carried over to the time of non-production and the staples and delicacies of any country may be exchanged for those of any other. No single discovery has contributed more to modern food manufacture nor to the general welfare of mankind.

Fig I.

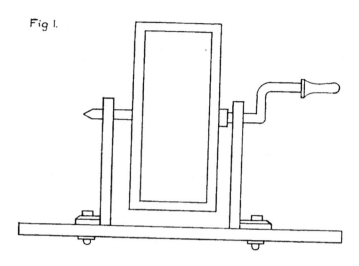

Fig. 2.

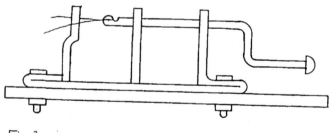

Fig. 3.

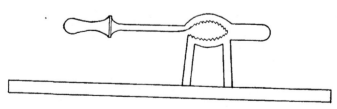

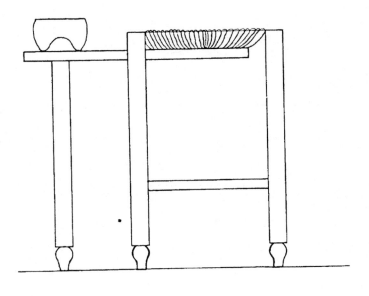

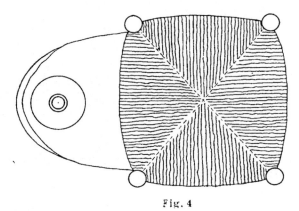

Fig. 4

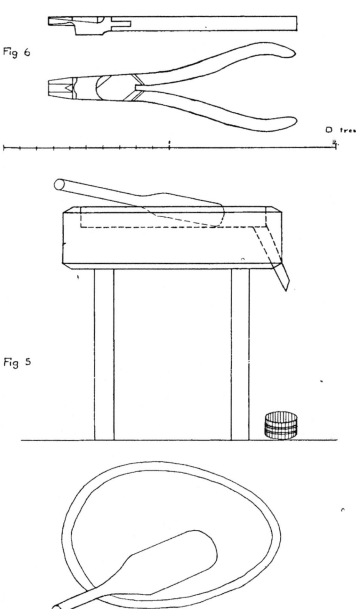

Fig 6

O tres

Fig 5

EXPLANATION OF THE PLATES

Perfect closing being of the greatest importance to obtain preservation of all alimentary substances, in order to attain it, I make use of the apparatus figured on the following plate, which, though susceptible of improvement, has answered my purpose perfectly. Consequently, I believe an explanation of it should be given.

First Figure. Reel with two iron wings used to double the wire which is afterwards cut in the middle by the reel, so as to have two lengths sufficient to fasten the corks in the bottles.

Second. Small machine to twist together for a third of their length the pieces of wire cut in two by the preceding machine.

Third. Iron vise used to compress and to reduce the corks for three-quarters of their length, starting at the smaller end.

Fourth. Straw-padded stool provided with a small wooden shelf upon which the bottles are placed so as to wire and to tie the corks more easily. The same stool may serve to set near the bottle-holder, when the closing is done.

Fifth. Block of wood, called bottle-holder, hollowed on its upper surface to form a shallow basin, in which the bottoms of the bottles are placed when they are to be corked. This block is provided with a strong wooden pallet, which is used to force the entrance of the stoppers.

Sixth. View of the front and side of a pliers, with a hinge-pin, which is used to twist the wire that holds the cork in and at the same time to cut the excess ends of wire.

As I shall indicate, I use the flat pliers and the shears for this operation.

The
Art of Preserving

ANIMAL AND VEGETABLE SUBSTANCES FOR MANY YEARS

Work submitted to the Consulting Bureau of Arts and Manufactures, invested with its approval, and published upon the invitation of His Excellency, the Minister of the Interior.

By APPERT,

Proprietor at Massy, Department of the Seine and Oise, former confectioner and distiller, elevated to be provisioner to the ducal house of Christian IV.

"I have thought that your discovery merited a particular testimonial of the good will of the Government."
Letter from His Excellency, the Minister of the Interior.

At the house of Patris & Co., Printers-Booksellers. Quay Napoleon, at the corner of the Street of the Dove, No. 4.

The author has complied with all that the law requires in order to guarantee his ownership; in consequence he serves notice that he will prosecute counterfeiters and dealers in counterfeit copies; and that any copy that does not bear his signature will be considered counterfeit.

Appert. (Signed).

CAUTION

By the Publisher

In order to avoid the imitations which might occur in the manufacture of preserved substances, advertised as from the manufactory at Massy, we have just made arrangements with M. Appert which we take the liberty of announcing to the public, that there will be found in our stores, Napoleon Quay, at the corner of the Street of the Dove, number 4, in the city, Paris, an assortment of preserved foods from the manufactory at Massy, at moderate prices and which may be determined from a list that we shall publish from time to time in the newspapers.

N. B. As these articles cannot be prepared in quantity, Messrs., the chefs for the admirals of the fleet and the staff, who desire to provision for long voyages are requested to make their orders in advance.

PREFACE

The art of preserving for many years animal and vegetable substances in all their freshness and with all their natural properties is not one of the doubtful discoveries set forth merely for interest and covetousness.

My method, exempt from all the objections with which all those used until now might justly be reproached, has received the sanction of a long experience; it is strengthened by the testimony of men skilled in the art and by the approbation of numerous consumers.

The principle of which I make use is unique; it operates in the same way and produces the same effects upon all foods without exception.

An illustrious minister, an ardent friend of the arts and of humanity, after having had my process verified by a special commission, has been pleased to accord encouragement to it which re-

doubled my zeal; but the most flattering
reward that could be accorded to me
is the invitation to render public, by way
of print, the knowledge of my process,
my discovery which may be of great usefulness in sea voyages, in hospitals, and
in domestic economy.

N. B. I shall receive with gratitude the observations that may be made upon my processes, and I shall hasten to give all the information that might be further desired after the
reading of this work; I only request perfect
frankness from those who address letters to me.

THE MINISTER OF THE INTERIOR

Court of the Empire,

to

M. Appert,

Proprietor at Massy, near Paris.

PARIS, January 30, 1810.

Second Division

Bureau of Arts and Manufactures.

The Consulting Bureau of Arts and Manufactures, has rendered an account to me, Sir, of the examination that it has made of your processes for the preservation of fruits, vegetables, meats, broths, milk, etc.; after this report one cannot doubt the reality of these processes. As the preservation of animal and vegetable substances can be of the greatest usefulness in sea voyages, in hospitals, and in domestic economy, I have felt that your discovery merited a special testimonial of the good-will of the Government. I have, in consequence, welcomed the proposition that has been made to me by the consulting bureau of according to you a reward of twelve thousand francs. In making this decision, I have had in view, at first, of awarding to you the recompense due to those who are originators of useful processes; afterwards to indemnify you for the expenses that you have been obliged to make to establish your workrooms, to devote yourself to the necessary experiments to verify the results of your methods. You shall immediately inform the chief of the division of accounts of my department the day when you desire to present yourself at the public treasury to receive the twelve thousand francs that I have accorded to you.

It has appeared to me, Sir, that it is important to spread the knowledge of your processes for the preservation of animal and vegetable substances. I desire, therefore, conformably to the proposal that you have made, that you write an exact and detailed description of these processes, that you deliver this description to the Consulting Bureau of Arts and Manufactures to be printed at your expense. After that it will be examined and reviewed. You are then to send two hundred copies to me. The delivery of these copies being the only condition that I place on the payment of the twelve thousand francs that you have been granted. I doubt not but that you will comply with this readily. I desire, Sir, that you acknowledge the receipt of my letter.

Accept the assurance of my distinguished sentiments.

(Signed)   Montalivet.

Consulting Bureau of Arts and Manufactures.

"The undersigned, members of the Consulting Bureau of Arts and Manufactures, next to the minister of the interior, charged by His Excellency to examine the description of the processes which are employed by M. Appert, for the preservation of foods, have recognized that the details which it includes on the manner of working and upon the results that are obtained, are accurate and conform to the various experiments that have been made on them before by M. Appert, by the order of His Excellency."

Paris, this 19th day of April, 1810.
Bardel, Gay-Lussac, Scipion-
                Perier, Molard.

————

Copy of a letter to General Caffarelli, Naval Prefect at Brest, by the Bureau of Health, under the date of the month of Brumaire, year 12.

"The foods prepared according to the process of Citizen Appert and sent to this port by the Minister of Marine, after a sojourn of three months upon the roadstead, presented the following condition:

The broth in bottles was good, the broth with boiled beef in a special vessel, good also, but weak; the boiled beef itself very edible.

The beans and small peas, prepared both with and without meat, have all the freshness and the agreeable flavor of freshly picked vegetables."

Signed Dubreuil, Billard, Duret, Pichon, and Thaumer.

A true copy.

The Secretary of the Council,

J. Miriel.

SOCIETY

FOR ENCOURAGEMENT

of National Industry

PARIS, April 7, 1809.

The Secretary of the Society for Encouragement of National Industry,

To M. Appert, Proprietor at Massy.

Sir:

I have the pleasure of transmitting to you a copy of the report made to the Society for Encouragement by Messrs. Guyton - Morveau, Parmentier, and Bouriat, upon your preserves of animal and vegetable substances. Nothing can be added to the judgment that the commission has made upon your discovery;

it announces, however, that it has not made experiments sufficiently rigorous nor continued for a sufficiently long time, to establish undeniably just at what point the substances that you prepare are susceptible of being preserved; but that which has been observed, has sufficed for it to form a conclusion already favorably disposed through the numerous and decisive testimonials which attest your success.

The Society for Encouragement believes it is of service to the country and to humanity in publishing, with the commendations which it merits, a discovery so generally useful. Its desires are accomplished, if its approbation, in leading the consumers to make use of your products, shall contribute to your obtaining just recompense for your work.

Accept, Sir, the assurance of the perfect consideration with which I have the honor to salute you.

Math. Montmorency, Sec. Adj.

THE ART OF

PRESERVING ANIMAL AND

VEGETABLE SUBSTANCES

All the imaginable means heretofore used for preserving foods or medicines are reduced to two principal methods; one in which desiccation is employed, the other in which more or less of a characteristic foreign substance is added to prevent fermentation and putrefaction. It is in following the first of these methods that dried fruits and vegetables, smoked meats, and salted fish are obtained. By the second are obtained fruits and different parts of vegetables preserved in sugar; juices and decoctions of plants reduced to syrups or in extracts; vegetables, fruits, and buds preserved in vinegar; meats, herbs, and vegetables salted; but all those means

(1)

carry more or less objection. Drying destroys the aroma, changes the flavor of the juices, shrivels the fibrous tissue or parenchyma. Whatever may be the savor, even in those which are very sapid, the sugar masks and destroys in part other savors, the presence of which it is desired to preserve, such as the agreeable acidity of many fruits. A second objection is that a great deal of sugar is required in order to preserve a small quantity of any other vegetable matter, and upon this account it is not only very costly but also detrimental in some cases. It is in the same manner that juices of plants cannot be reduced to the form of syrups or extracts without at least nearly double the quantity of sugar; this results in the syrups or extracts containing much more of the sugar than of the medicament, and oftimes the sugar darkens to the detriment and the action of the medicine.

The salt carries into the substance a disagreeable harshness, hardens the animal fibre there, and renders it indigestible (1); it contracts vegetable parenchyma. On the other hand, as it is necessary to remove the major part of the salt used by means of water, nearly all the soluble principles in the cold water are lost when soaking is done; there remains only the fibrous or parenchymatous matter, which, as has been said, is also altered.

---

(1) "The salted meats, upon which the ships' crews are fed, appear to be the principal cause of scurvy; it seems that the same reasons which cause salts to prevent the fermentation of meats, render them difficult of digestion. Though a small quantity of salt may be able to check putrefaction, the too abundant and too continued use made of it, may produce derangement in the fine ducts, and these derangements cannot fail to over-work the stomach of persons who have to digest dried vegetables and the biscuits which aged sailors cannot masticate thoroughly. Poor digestion and obstruction of the small vessels may occasion ulcers of the mouth, and the spots which denote scurvy, etc."

(Sante des Marins, par Duhamel, page 64.)

The vinegar can only serve as seasoning for many substances.

I shall not enter into detail upon all that has been said and published on the art of preserving foods; these works are known. I shall only observe that not to my knowledge, has any author, ancient or modern, indicated, nor even surmised, the principle that forms the basis of the method which I offer.

It is well known that for some time at Paris and in the provinces, public attention was directed towards means of diminishing the consumption of sugar and in making up the deficiency by various extracts of native substances. The Government whose philanthropic oversight is extended to all useful subjects, is unremitting in inviting those who are concerned in the arts and sciences to determine means of most advantageously turning to account the productions from our soil, and giving the greatest development to agriculture and to our manufactures so as to lessen the consumption of foreign merchandise. In order to contribute to the same end the Society for Encouragement of National Industry inspired by flattering rewards those whose talents and efforts were directed toward discoveries, from which the nation and humanity might draw real advantages. Animated by as laudable a zeal, the Society of Agriculture through its resolution of the 21st of June, 1809, and its circular of the following 15th of July, made a general appeal so as to obtain directions and information that might serve in the composition of a work upon the art of preserving all alimentary substances by the best possible means.

It is following these invitations so deserving of respect, that I decided to publish a method, easy to put in practise, and particularly at little cost in its execution, a method, which by the extension to which it is susceptible, may present numerous advantages to the society.

This method is not an empty theory; it is the fruit of my vigils, of my meditation, of research, and of numerous experiments, the results of which after more than ten years, have produced such wonder that, notwithstanding the evidence acquired from the repeated use of preserved edibles, for two, three, and six years, many persons still do not believe in it.

Reared in the art of preparing and preserving by these processes, I knew alimentary products; having lived, as it were, in pantries, in breweries, in store-rooms, and in the cellars of Champagne, as well as in the factories of the confectioners and distillers, and in the store-houses of the grocers; accustomed to superintend and to conduct establishments of this kind during forty-five years, I have been able to give a faithful account of my work, aided by numerous advantages which could not be procured by the majority of those who are occupied with the art of preserving foods.

I owe to my experiments and above all to a great perseverance, to being convinced, 1st, that the subject of heat has the essential quality in itself not only of changing the combination of the constituent parts of animal and vegetable products, but also that, if not destroying, at least of arresting for many years the natural tendency of these same products to decomposition; 2nd, that its application in a proper manner to all these products, after having deprived them in the most rigorous manner possible of contact with the air, effects perfect preservation of these same products with all their natural qualities.

Before entering into the details of the execution of my process, I ought to say that it consists principally:

1st. To enclose in the bottle or jar the substances that one wishes to preserve;

2d. To cork these different vessels with the greatest care because success depends chiefly on the closing;

3d. To submit these substances thus enclosed to the action of boiling water in a water-bath for more or less time according to their nature and in the manner that I shall indicate for each kind of food;

4th. To remove the bottles from the water-bath at the time prescribed.

————

*Description of the manufactories that I
have established for the execution of
my process on a large scale* (1)

My laboratory consists of four compartments or workshops. The first furnished with a battery of kitchen utensils,
of stoves, and of the necessary apparatus
for preparing all the animal substances
intended to be preserved, such as a marmite for consommés, of thirty weltes (*)
capacity, mounted in masonry. This
marmite is furnished with a double
boiler pierced with small openings like
a colander, having compartments intended to admit meats and fowl, which

---

(1) One understands that for special use
in the home and for small operations, it is
unnecessary to establish workrooms; the vessels and other utensils which are found wher-
ever economical housekeepers occupy themselves with their winter provisions, suffice for
working according to my method.

(*) Welte—velt? Mauritian liquid measure,
2 gallons or 7.57 liters.

are introduced in the first, and this withdrawn at will with all the meats.

The first is equipped with a strong valve to which is applied in the interior of the marmite a small ball, like that of a watering pot, covered with a piece of bolting cloth. By this means the bouillon or consommé is obtained clear and all ready to put in bottles.

The second piece is intended for preparing milk, cream, and whey.

The third for corking, wiring, and placing in sacking the bottles and other vessels.

The fourth is furnished with three large copper kettles mounted in masonry on the furnaces. Each of these kettles is furnished with a strong cover just large enough to enter the inside and rest upon the vessels. Each boiler is equipped with a strong valve at the bottom to let out the water at proper times; these vessels generally receive all the objects that are intended to be preserved, so as to apply to them in a suitable manner the action of the heat of the water-bath. (1.)

---

(1) However in extensive operations, it is necessary to have the large boilers equipped with strong valves as otherwise they would be too long in cooling with such a volume of water, and resting during the time on a hot furnace; on the other hand the heat applied for too long a time might greatly injure the substances. In small operations and in homes the first kettle or earthenware vessel would serve, therefore, without inconvenience, provided that the bottles be immersed just to the cord line or ring; one could even in default of so tall a vessel, lay them in the water-bath taking the precaution to pack them well there so as to avoid breaking. Many operations handled in this way have succeeded very well with me. The corks work out a little farther, but if the bottles be well corked, there is nothing to fear. For example, it is not advisable to use vessels closed with corks made of several pieces, because these corks are strained more by the action of the heat, and however well closed the vessel may be, it would be imprudent to use them.

The utensils which furnish the third piece for the preparatory processes consist:

1. Of pieces of boards to set between the bottles.

2. Of a reel for the wire intended to bind the bottles and other vessels. (Fig. 1.)

3. Of shears and pliers for wiring. (Fig. 6.)

4. Of a small lathe for twisting the wire when it is cut into lengths. (Fig. 2).

5. Of a vise for squeezing the corks. (Fig. 3.)

6. Of a bottle - holder or block mounted on three legs, furnished with a strong pallet for corking. (Fig. 5.)

The small water-baths are so much more convenient since they can be placed anywhere, and charged at will; they cool promptly and when one can hold his hand within, the bottles are withdrawn, and the operation is therefore terminated.

7. Of a stool mounted on five legs for wiring. (Fig. 4.)

8. Of a sufficient quantity of sacking to envelop the bottles and other vessels.

9. Of two leather-covered stools, stuffed with hay, upon which to rest the bottles when it is necessary to press down the contents.

10. Of a press for the juices of plants, fruits, herbs, and the must of grapes, with the earthenware, vessels, sieve, and all the other necessary things.

In addition to this laboratory, equipped in this manner, I have established three workshops; the first, for preparing the vegetables, which is furnished with tables round the outer walls.

The second for receiving and preparing the fruit, received from the greengrocer.

The third is a cellar furnished with board staging, used for rinsing and compactly arranging the bottles and other vessels in storage.

I take the precaution to rinse in advance the bottles and vessels which I expect to need. I procure an assortment of corks, which I squeeze, also wire which I lay out; when all are thus prepared, the operations are half done.

The principle of preservation of all foods is invariable in its effect; the results depend entirely on its application in a suitable measure to each of them according to their nature, and with the exclusion of air. This last precaution is of the greatest importance in order to attain perfect preservation. A sure means of depriving the foods from contact with air, is to have a perfect understanding of the bottles and vessels which are used, of the corks, and of the method of good closing.

BOTTLES AND VESSELS

I have chosen glass as being the material most impermeable to air. I have not risked a trial with other materials. The ordinary bottles generally have the openings too small and are poorly made; they are too weak in other respects to resist the blows of the pallet and the action of the heat. Therefore I have had bottles made expressly, having larger openings and with contractions, that is to say, with a ridge extending into the interior of the opening below the cord-line (or ring). My object was that the cork introduced with force upon the bottle-holder, of which I have spoken, with the assistance of the pallet, up to three-quarters of its length, was constricted through the middle. In this manner the bottle is found perfectly closed to the exterior and equally so to the interior. This opposes therefore an obstacle to the expansion which is produced upon the substances enclosed in the bottle, by the application of heat.

This manner of closing is so much the more indispensable, since I have observed many times that the expansion was so strong that it forced out the corks two, three, and four *lignes* (1), though secured by two cross wires. The bottles and jars should be of lightly tempered material, the former twenty-five to twenty-six ounces in weight for a liter capacity, in which the glass be distributed equally; otherwise they break in the water-bath at the place where they are charged heaviest with matter. The form used for Champagne is the most suitable, the best looking, permits better arrangement, and is more resistive than the others.

STOPPERS.

It is in general poor economy, due to misapprehension, that of paying only twenty and even forty sols (2) for a

---

(1)   Ligne—0.08″
(2)   Sol—5 centimes (one cent American money)

hundred corks, though having the allure-
ment of two centimes that you believe
gained upon a cork, you often sacrifice
by this parsimony a bottle of 20, 30s, and
even of three pounds and over. The bottles are corked so as to preserve and im-
prove the object enclosed, in depriving
it of contact with the air; one cannot
then give too much care to the good quality of the stoppers, which should be 18
to 20 lignes in length and of the finest
cork; these are really the most economical. Experiment has proved this so
true, that as for myself I use only superfine corks for all work. I also take the
precaution of compressing each cork for
three-quarters of its length, by means
of the vise (Fig. 3), beginning at the
smaller end; in compressing in this manner, the cork becomes more supple, the
pores are brought closer together, the
stopper is slightly elongated and reduced in size at the end that enters the
mouth of the bottle, so that a large stopper may enter into an average opening.

The action of the heat in a vessel thus closed is such that the enlarged stopper in the interior of the vessel makes a perfect closure.

CLOSURE.

After what has been said, the absolute necessity of having good bottles is understood, the material of which should be distributed uniformly and with a small thread extending into the interior of the opening. It is also necessary to have superfine stoppers, pressed for three-quarters of their length by the vise. Before putting in the corks, I am careful that the bottles containing liquid are filled only to three inches of the cordline (or ring), so as to avoid the breakage that would necessarily follow from the expansion produced by the application of the heat in the water-bath if the bottles were too full; as for vegetables, fruits, plants, etc., two inches from the ring or cordline suffice. I place the full bottle upon the bottle-holder, already cited, before which I am seated. This

apparatus should be provided with a
strong wooden pallet with a small jug
full of water, and a well sharpened
knife, greased with a little tallow or
soap so as to cut the heads of corks,
which ought rarely to be found extending beyond the exterior of the bottle.
The objects arranged, I draw the bottle-
holder between my legs, and introduce
into the bottle a suitable stopper after
having wet half of it in the vessel of
water, so that it may enter more easily,
and after having wiped the end, I press
it in this position with my left hand
which I hold steady so that the bottle
may be perpendicular. I take the pallet
with my right hand so as to push the
cork in with force. When I feel after
the first or second blow that the cork
has entered a little, I stop so as to take
the neck of the bottle in that hand, which
I hold firm and perpendicular upon the
bottle holder, and with repeated blows
of the p a l l e t I continue forcing the
stopper in to three-fourths of its length.
The quarter of the stopper which

should always extend beyond the bottle after having resisted the repeated blows of the pallet assures me on the one hand that the bottle is closed perfectly, and on the other hand this excess is necessary for the cork to support the two crossed wires or two strings, so as to hold it against the compression which it experiences in the water-bath. One cannot be too careful in attaining a good closure; no small details should be neglected in order that the substance which is to be preserved should be rigorously excluded from contact with the air since it is the destructive agent most to be feared. (1.)

---

(1) Many persons believe that they have made a good closing when the cork is forced level with the mouth of the bottle, but it is quite the contrary; the general rule, when the cork does not resist the repeated blows of a strong pallet, and is pushed entirely into the bottle, is that it is always prudent to withdraw it and substitute another more suitable. Thus to believe that a bottle closed so low is properly closed,

The bottles thus properly closed, I
further secure the stoppers by two

---

though it does not come out on reversing it, is
a mistake which, joined to the poor quality of
the corks that are used, cause much loss. He
who corks with care is assured of good closure
by the resistance of the stopper to the blows of
the pallet, and reversing the bottle is never to
be considered. On the other hand it is not only
necessary to give consideration to the openings
that are found in the cork but to all the hidden
defects that may exist in the interior of
even the finest, defects through which the
air may be introduced, so that it is felt to be
an indispensable necessity to use only the best
corks possible, after having squeezed them
properly in the vise, and to make the closing
sufficiently strong so that the corks may be tied
through the middle, in order to avoid infinite
losses that have no other cause than that of poor
closing; for if a bottle that has been closed with
lack of care does not leak at the moment, it is
because the air has not had time to penetrate
through the defects that may exist; but likewise, in practise, how much variety in the quality of a wine drawn from the same puncheon!
how much in the bottles from more or less of
the lees! etc.

crossed wires (this is very easy, it suffices to have seen it once). Afterwards I put each bottle in a sackcloth or coarse canvas, made expressly, and large enough to envelop the whole up to the stopper. These sacks are made like a muff, opening equally through the two ends, one of which is gathered with a running string, leaving an opening only the size of a five franc piece. The other end is provided with two strings so as to hold the sack round the neck of the bottle. By means of these sacks, I can dispense with hay or straw in packing the bottles in the water-bath, and when one is broken in the operation, which happens sometimes, the fragments of the broken bottles remain in the sacking. I thus avoid an infinity of embarrassments and small accidents that are experienced in gathering the splinters of bottles scattered in the hay or straw, with which I had to contend in former times.

After having spoken of the bottles, their form and quality, of the stoppers,

the length and the fine cork from which
they should be made, of the manner of
proper closing, as well as that of tying,
of the sacking, its form and use, I shall
give an idea of the vessels with large
openings, that is to say, of the jars of
glass which have openings of 2, 3, and 4
inches and more in diameter, and of more
or less capacity, that I use for preserving large objects, such as meats, fowl,
game, fish, eggs, etc. These jars are,
like the bottles, provided with a cordline (or ring), not only for re-enforcing
the opening, but also for receiving the
wire used to hold the stoppers. I have
not yet been able to obtain from the
glass-makers a small thread extending
into the interior, like that in the bottles.
The closing of these jars, because of
this defect, is more difficult, and requires
special care. The cork produces still
another impediment, especially the very
fine, when the sheets are too fine and
wrongly constructed by having the
pores ascending. It has necessitated
forming the stoppers of 3, 4, and 5 lay-

ers of cork of 20 to 24 *lignes* in height, glued with good sense, that is to say, the pores of the cork placed horizontally, with fish glue, prepared in the following manner:

I have dissolved four *gros* (1) of well-beaten fish glue in eight ounces of water over the fire; when dissolved, it was strained through fine cloth, then put back on the fire so as to reduce it to a third of its volume, after which an ounce of good brandy of twenty-two degrees was added. I have left the whole over the fire until reduced to about three ounces. The glue, thus prepared, was put in a small pot over the hot ashes, then the sheets of cork, carefully heated, were lightly coated with a brush, so as to glue them together; a string was passed to the two extremities of the cork, so as to hold the sheets lightly squeezed, and allow them to dry either in the sun or hanging in a gentle heat for about 15 days. At the end of that time, I have,

---

(1) Gros—⅛ ounce.

with a cork-cutting knife, given the proper form to the corks, and have cut them to fit each mouth exactly; they have been very successful for me. After having closed the jars and pushed the stoppers in by force with the aid of the pallet, and always perpendicular on the bottle-holder, I treat them with a luting compound. This lute, the composition imparted to me by M. Bardel, made of quicklime, is exposed to the air after being sprinkled with water to dissolve and reduce it to a powder. It is held in closed bottles or jars until needed. This lime, mixed to a white cheese, *a la pie,* to the consistency of paste, produces a lute which hardens rapidly and which resists the heat of boiling water. With this lute the exterior of the cork is c o a t e d , the edge of the jars wrapped with hemp and with small bands of cloth above, is properly supported against the cork, and descending from it to the cordline (or ring). Afterwards, so that the wire would be able to hold with greater force in maintaining the cork, I have placed a piece of cork 7 to 8 *lignes* in height, 16 to 18 in diameter in the center of a cork too large to have the wire have effect. At the center of this second cork, applied at the center of the large one, I succeeded in making the wire hold with force and give the proper reinforcement to the cork.

When everything is foreseen and prepared, particularly properly closed, wired, and enveloped in the sacking, one has only to bestow upon all these substances thus prepared the application of the preservation principle. This final part is the most easily done.

All the vessels or bottles are arranged upright in a boiler which is filled afterward with fresh water, so that the vessels are covered to the cordline (or ring). The boiler is closed with its cover, which is set on the vessels; over the cover is placed a wet cloth so as to close all outlets and prevent, as far as possible, evaporation from the water-bath. As soon as the boiler is prepared in this manner, the fire is placed under it; when the water-bath is at boiling or ebullition, the same degree of heat is continued for more or less time, according to the nature of the contained objects. At the end of the time the fire is promptly removed into an extinguisher. A quarter of an hour after the fire is removed, the water is released through the valve; a half-hour after the water is removed, the boiler is uncovered; the work is completed when the bottles or vessels are taken out one or two hours after opening. The following day, or fifteen days after (it is immaterial), the bottles are arranged upon laths, like wine, in a temperate and shaded place; if the expectation is to send them to a distance, it is necessary to tar them before putting them on the laths, otherwise this last operation may be dispensed with; the bottles have also been laid upon a ladder for three years, the substances having as much savor as when they were prepared, and yet they had not been tarred.

It can be seen from the preceding that all foods that one desires to preserve should be subjected, without exception, to the application of the heat of the water-bath in a manner suitable to each of them, after having been excluded rigorously from contact with air by the care and the processes that have been indicated.

The principle of preservation is invariable in its effects, as I have already observed. So that all the losses that I have experienced in my operations have no other cause than that of bad application of the principle, or of forgetfulness or negligence in the preparatory processes, according to the account of them that I have rendered. It happens sometimes that I do not have entire success in my operations; but who is the worker who never makes a mistake? May one flatter himself that he can constantly avoid loss that may be caused by a defect existing in a vessel, perhaps in the interior of a cork, etc.? In truth, these cases are extremely rare, when there is attention given.

*Means of distinguishing on taking from
the boiler the bottles or jars which, by
reason of some accidental cause or
through the action of heat, or through
lack of attention in the preparatory
processes, risk being spoiled.*

Each operation terminated, irrespec-
tive of what kind, the greatest care is
taken to examine with the most minute
attention all the bottles in taking them,
one after the other, from the boiler.

I have observed those with defects in
the glass, as stars and cracks, occasioned
by the action of the heat of the water-
bath, or by the wiring when the mouth
of the vessel is too weak, others which
show by a slight moisture around the
cork or by small spots at the mouth that
the enclosed substance had filtered out
at the moment of expansion from the
application of heat in the water-bath;
these are the two principal observations

that I have made; as soon as I have discovered any bottles with these defects, that I am certain cannot be preserved, they are put aside to make use of later, so that nothing be lost.

The first cause of damage that I wish to point out pertains to the quality and the poor manufacture of bottles; but the second may proceed, first, from a poor cork; second, having a poor mouth; third, having the bottle too full; fourth and finally, having bad tying, etc. One alone of these faults suffices to lose a bottle, with greater reason when there is a complication.

In the application of heat in the water-bath many obstacles are encountered, particularly for small peas; because, of all foods, they are the most difficult to preserve perfectly. This vegetable, if gathered too tender or too small, dissolves in water, the bottle is found only half full, and this half is not even fit to preserve (when by chance I discover them in this condition, they are carefully set aside, so as to make use of them later). If the small peas have been gathered for two or three days, they have lost all their flavor on account of the heat; they harden, they ferment before the operation, the bottles break with detonation in the water-bath; those which resist breaking successively or are defective, can be easily recognized by the juice found in the bottle, which is turbid, instead of which the properly preserved small peas have clear juice.

It is not necessary to recommend celerity and the greatest cleanliness in the preparation of foods; this is indispensable, particularly for those which are to be preserved.

All necessary arrangements are made in advance, so that nothing be delayed and that all the time may be used to advantage.

Description of the processes which constitute my method; its special and particular application to each of the substances that one desires to preserve.

POT-AU-FEU.

I make the customary soup; when the meat has three-quarters cooked, half of it that had been boned is taken out so as to preserve it. The soup made, the broth from it is strained; after it has cooled, it is put in bottles, which have been properly closed, tied, and each one wrapped in sacking. The beef, three-quarters cooked, which was removed, is put in wide-mouthed bottles covered with some of the same broth. After having properly closed, luted, tied, and put them in sacking, they are placed upright in a boiler with the bottles containing the soup; the boiler is filled with fresh water, so that the bottles and jars are covered up to the cordline (or ring);

the cover is placed on the boiler, making it set over the vessels, after having carefully wrapped it with the wet cloth so as to close all outlets and prevent, as far as possible, evaporation from the water-bath; then fire is put under the boiler; when the water-bath has been in ebullition or up to boiling, the same degree of heat is maintained for an hour, after which the fire is carefully removed in an extinguisher. A half-hour after, the water is let out from the water-bath through the valve which is found in the base of the boiler; at the end of another half-hour, the boiler is uncovered; an hour or two after the opening of the boiler (the time is immaterial—it depends more or less on the care which the boiler requires), the bottles and jars are removed; the stoppers are coated the following day with white resin, so as to send them out to various seaports. At the end of a year or eighteen months, the soup and the meat have been found as good as if made the same day.

CONSOMME

In the year 12, having hopes of furnishing the supplies for the invalids on board His Majesty's vessels, after having made various experiments in seaports, by order of His Excellency, the Minister of Marine and the Colonies, upon food products preserved by my method, I made the necessary arrangements to respond to the demands on which I had occasion to count. Consequently, in order to have less multiplication of jars, and to be able to put eight liters of soup in a bottle, I made the following experiment. Usually, as evaporation is conducted only at the expense of the object which it is desired to dry, (1) I have prepared a dark con-

---

(1) Jellies, meat essences, the foundation of glacés, and bouillon tablets, which are obtained from the soft white parts of animals, with the help of the horns of deer and of fish glue, preserved until hard by means of evaporation

sommé from two pounds of good meat and fowl per liter. The consommé being made, strained, and cooled, is put in bottles. Then having been properly closed, tied, and put in sacking, it is placed in the boiler. The best pieces of beef and fowl are removed when a quarter cooked. When these pieces had cooled, they were put in large-mouthed bottles and the meat covered with the same consommé. After having properly closed, luted, wired, and put in sacking, they were placed upright in the same boiler with the bottles of consommé. Having filled the boiler with cold water to the cordline (or ring) of the vessels, and having covered and provided the cover with a wet cloth, the fire is put under the water-bath. When it reaches the boiling point, this degree of heat is continued for two hours, and the opera-

---

through drying in stoves, offer only artificial maintenance, without savor and without taste other than that of empyreuma and of mustiness, etc.

tion finished like the preceding. The beef and the fowl, as well as the consommé, were found suitably cooked and preserved for more than two years.

BOUILLON OR PECTORAL JELLY

This jelly is prepared according to the prescription of a physician, with calves' lungs and feet and a sufficient quantity of red cabbage, carrots, turnips, onions, and leeks; a quarter of an hour before taking the jelly from the fire, candied sugar with Senegal gum are added. It is strained as soon as made, after which it is cooled, put in bottles, closed, tied, enveloped in sacking, and placed in the water-bath for a quarter of an hour's boiling, etc. The jelly was perfectly preserved, besides being as good as if it had been made today.

FILET OF BEEF, MUTTON, FOWL, AND PARTRIDGE.

All of these substances have been prepared just as for daily use, but only three-quarters cooked, in the same manner as roasted partridges. When all have cooled, they are put separately into wide-mouthed bottles. After having been properly closed, luted, tied, and put in sacking, all are placed in the water-bath so as to give a half-hour's boiling, etc. These substances were sent to Brest, where they have been put in the sea for four months and ten days with preserved vegetables, consommé, and milk, the whole well packed in a chest. When the opening was made, all the substances, eighteen in number, were tasted. They were found with all their freshness, and not a single jar was found showing alteration from the sea.

To these four experiments, I have added two others that I have done—one on a fricassee of chicken, and the other on a matelote of eels, carp, and pike, garnished with veal sweetbreads, mushrooms, onions, and anchovy butter, the whole cooked in white wine. The chicken fricassee and the matelote were preserved perfectly.

These results prove sufficiently that the same principle applied through the same preparatory processes, with the same care and precautions, in general, preserve all animal productions, being mindful not to give any of them in preparation more than three-quarters cooking at the most, so as to give the additional cooking in the water-bath.

Most of these substances, such as bouillon, consommé, the jellies, and the essences of meats, fowl, and ham, the juices of plants, the must and syrup of grapes, etc., are able to stand an hour's boiling or more in the water-bath without any danger, but to many of the others a quarter of an hour, even a minute, too long would be injurious. Thus the results are always subordinate to the intelligence, the celerity and the knowledge of the manipulator (1).

---

(1) "One does not speak in the workrooms (said the celebrated Chaptal, Elements of chemistry, preliminary discourse, p. XXXI.)

FRESH EGGS.

The freshest eggs are most resistive to the heat of the water-bath; in consequence, I have taken the day's eggs, which are arranged in a short-necked bottle with raspings of bread to fill the spaces and to guarantee the eggs from breaking during the voyages. The bottles are properly closed, luted, tied, etc. They are put into a large kettle of suf-

---

because of the caprices of the operations; but it appears that this vague statement has taken birth in the ignorance in which the workers are of the true principles of their art; because nature is not influenced by determination and discernment; it obeys constant laws. The dead matter which we employ in our workshops, presents the requisite effects in which the will has no part, and in which consequently it could not know nor have caprices. *"Know better your original materials,"* could be said to the workmen, *"study better the principles of your art, and you can foresee all, predict all, and calculate all; it is only your ignorance that makes of your operations a continual groping, and a dis-*

ficient size (1) so as to give them 60 and 90 degrees heat. Afterward the water-bath is removed from the fire; when it has cooled so that the hand can be held in it, the eggs are removed from it and kept six months. At the end of that pe-

---

couraging alternative of success and reverse." In short, the manipulator who works with a perfect knowledge of the principles of his art and of the result of its application, will be surprised and astonished by a loss or a reverse that he may experience in his operations, and far from attributing it to caprice, will discover the cause of this loss to be the neglect of some necessary precaution in the application of the same principle; the reverses will serve him as standards to better calculate and perfect the preparatory processes. As he acquires the conviction of the invariability of his principle in its effects, he knows that all loss or reverse can only proceed from poor application.

(1) This operation on a large scale, that is to say, in a large boiler, will require more care, in that it is more difficult to control the degree of heat than in a small water-bath which is changed at will.

riod, the eggs are taken out of the bottle; they are placed on the fire in fresh water to which 60 to 90 degrees of heat are given. They were cooked properly for the sippet, and also as fresh as when they had been prepared. As for the hard eggs, treated *a la tripe* or *a la blanche sauce,* etc., they are given 80 degrees of heat in the water-bath, that is to say, when the boiling starts, they are removed from the fire.

MILK.

Twelve liters of milk fresh from the cow have been taken, set in the water-bath and reduced to two-thirds of its volume, skimming it often. Afterwards it is strained through cloth; when cooled, the skin which had formed on it in cooling is removed, and the milk is put in bottles with the ordinary processes, and then in the water-bath for two hours' boiling, etc. At the end of some months it was noticed that the cream had separated in flakes and was floating on the surface in the bottle. In order to avoid this objection, a second experiment was made with an equal quantity of milk which had been reduced in the water-bath by a half instead of a third, as in the first. I conceived adding to it, when it was reduced, eight fresh egg yolks diluted wth the same milk. After having left the whole thus well mixed a half-hour over the fire, it was finished as in the former experiment.

This method has succeeded perfectly. The egg yolks had so thickened it all that at the end of a year, and even eighteen months, the milk was preserved so that I have put it in bottles. The former was likewise preserved for two years and more; the cream which had formed in flakes disappeared on putting it on the fire, both of them tolerating the same heating. From both of them butter and whey were obtained; in the different experiments and chemical analyses to which they had been submitted it has been recognized that the latter, truly superior, could replace the best cream that is sold in Paris for coffee.

CREAM.

Five liters of cream, skimmed carefully from good milk, were concentrated without skimming to four liters in the water-bath, the skin which had formed on it was removed, so as to strain the whole through cloth, and put it to cool. After having again removed the skin that had formed in cooling, it was put into half-liter bottles with the ordinary processes, so as to give it an hour's boiling in the water-bath. At the end of two years this cream was found as fresh as if it had been prepared that day. I have made good fresh butter from it in quantities of 4 to 5 ounces per half-liter.

WHEY.

I have prepared whey by the ordinary processes in practise. When it was clarified and cooled, it was put in bottles, etc., so as to give it an hour's boiling in the water-bath. However well clarified the whey may be, when put in the water-bath, the application of the heat always separates from it some particles of cheese which form a deposit; I have kept it two to three years in this way, and before making use of it have filtered it so as to have it very clear. In case of haste, it suffices to decant it, to obtain it clear.

VEGETABLES.

As the difference in climate produces more or less early growth, and causes much variety in their qualities, their species, and their properties, one must be governed in consequence by the place in which they grow.

At Paris and in its environs, June and July are the best season for preserving small green peas, small broad beans, and asparagus. Later these vegetables lose too much through heat and dryness. In August and September I preserve artichokes, French and kidney beans, as well as cauliflowers. In general, all vegetables intended to be preserved should be gathered as late as possible and prepared with the greatest haste, so that there is only a step from the garden to the water-bath.

SMALL GREEN PEAS.

The *Clamard* and the *Crochu* are the two species of peas that I prefer, particularly the latter, which is the mellowest and the sweetest of all, as well as the earliest, after the *Michaux,* however, which is the earliest of all; but the latter is not suitable for preserving. I do not gather them too small, as they soften in the water during the operation; they are taken when of medium size as (being more advanced) they have much more taste and savor. They are shelled immediately on gathering. The largest ones are separated from these, after which they are carefully heaped in the bottles upon the bench already cited, so as to get in as many as possible. They

are closed, etc., so as to put them in the
water-bath in order to boil for an hour
and a half, when the season is cool and
moist, and two hours when it is hot and
dry; the operation is finished like the
preceding.

The large ones which have been separated from the smaller, are likewise
put in bottles; they are closed, etc., so as
to give them, according to the season,
two hours or two and a half hours boil-
in the water-bath.

ASPARAGUS.

The asparagus is cleaned as for daily
use, whether whole or in small pieces.
Before putting it into bottles or jars,
it is plunged into boiling water and
then into cold water, so as to remove the
acridity peculiar to this vegetable; the
whole ones are arranged carefully in
jars, the head at the bottom; those prepared in littles pieces are put in bottles.
After both are well drained, they are

closed, etc., and put in the water-bath so
as to receive there a boiling only, etc.

SMALL BROAD BEANS.

Neither the horse-bean, nor even the
Julienne, which greatly resembles it, is
good to preserve. I use the true broad
bean, which is as large as my thumb,
when it is mature. It is gathered very
small, the size of my little finger, for to
preserve the pod. As the pod is susceptible to contact with the air, which browns
it, the precaution is taken in shelling to
put these in the bottles. When the bottles are filled and heaped lightly on the
stool, and all the spaces filled, a small
boquet of savory is added to each bottle.
They are closed quickly, etc., so as to put
them in the water-bath to boil for an
hour, etc. When this vegetable is gathered, prepared, and manufactured with
celerity, it is obtained of a greenish
white; on the other hand, when slow in
preparation, it browns and hardens.

SHELLED BROAD BEANS.

To preserve the shelled broad beans, they are taken very large, about a half-inch or more in length; they are shelled and put in bottles with a small bouquet of savory, etc., and then put in the water-bath so as to boil for an hour and a half, etc.

FRENCH BEANS.

The kidney bean known under the name Bayolet, which resembles the Swiss, is the species which is better suited to preserve green; it unites the best taste with uniformity; I gather them as for daily use. As soon as picked, they are put immediately into bottles which are carefully heaped when on the bench so as to fill the spaces. They are closed, etc., and put in the water-bath for an hour and a half. When the beans are a little larger, they are cut lengthwise into two or three pieces; when cut this way, they need only an hour in the water-bath.

WHITE BEANS.

The kidney bean of Soissons merits the just title to preference; in default of it, I take the best possible, gathering them when the pod begins to yellow; they are shelled and put in bottles immediately, etc. They are put in the water-bath to boil for two hours, etc.

WHOLE ARTICHOKES.

I take them of average size; after having removed all the unnecessary leaves, and pared them, they are plunged into boiling water, and then into cold water; after they have drained, they are put in wide-mouthed bottles, closed, etc., and then in the water-bath to receive an hour's boiling, etc.

QUARTERED ARTICHOKES.

The fine artichokes are cut into eight pieces; the outer leaves are removed,

only a few being left. They are plunged
into boiling water, then into cold water;
when well drained, they are put on the
stove in a casserole, with a bit of fresh
butter, seasoning, and fine herbs; when
half-cooked, they are removed from the
stove and put to cool; then they are put
in wide-mouthed bottles, closed, luted,
tied, etc., and put in the water-bath to
boil for a half-hour, etc.

CAULIFLOWERS.

Like the artichokes, when the cauliflowers are well cleaned, they are plunged into boiling water, then into cold water; when they are well drained, they are
put into wide-mouthed bottles, etc.; they
are put in the water-bath so as to give
them a half-hour's boiling, etc.

As the years vary and are sometimes
dry, sometimes wet, one will readily see
that it is equally necessary to study and
to vary the degree of heat which is advisable under the two conditions; it is a

special consideration which should not be neglected.

For example in a cool and moist year, the vegetables are tenderer, and consequently more susceptible to the action of heat; in this case, 7 to 8 minutes less boiling in the water-bath should be given, and to give as much more in the dry years when the vegetables are firmer and more resistive to the action of heat, etc.

SORREL.

I have gathered sorrel, mountain spinach, lettuce, white beet, chervil, scallion, etc., in suitable amounts. When they are properly picked, washed, drained, and cut, the whole is cooked in a copper vessel well tinned. These vegetables should be cooked as for daily use, and not dried and scorched, as is often done in the home when they are to be preserved. This degree of cooking is most suitable. When the herb is prepared in this way, it is put to cool in earthenware or stoneware vessels; then put into bottles of somewhat large opening, closed, etc., and put in the water-bath to be given a quarter-hour's boiling only. This time suffices to preserve it intact for ten years and also as fresh as if it came from the garden. This way is without doubt the best and the most economical for homes, and civil and military hospitals. It is above all advantageous for the sailor; because it may be carried thus prepared, to farthest India, as fresh and as savory as though cooked that day.

SPINACH AND CHICORY.

These two kinds are prepared as for ordinary use; when they are newly gathered, cleaned, blanched, cooled, pressed, and minced, they are put in bottles, etc., so as to boil them a quarter of an hour in the water-bath, etc.

Carrots, cabbage, turnips, parsnips, onions, potatoes, celery, Spanish cardoons, beets, and in general all vegetables, are preserved alike, they may be blanched only, or prepared with or without meat according to the use made of them when taken out of the vessel. In the former case, the vegetables that are to be preserved, are blanched and half-cooked in water with a little salt; they are removed from the fire so as to drain and cool them; afterwards they are put into bottles, etc., so as to put them in the water-bath and give to the carrots, cabbage, turnips, parsnips, and beets an hour's boiling, and a half hour to the onions, potatoes, celery, etc. In the latter case the vegetables are prepared, with or without meat, as for ordinary use; when they are cooked three-quarters and properly prepared and seasoned, they are taken from the fire so as to let them cool; then put into bottles, closed, etc., so as to give a full quarter of an hour's boiling in the water-bath, etc.

JULIENNE.

A julienne soup of carrots, leeks, turnips, sorrel, French beans, celery, little peas, etc., was prepared in the ordinary way, which consists of cutting into small pieces either round or long, carrots, turnips, leeks, French beans, and celery. After having properly picked and washed them, the vegetables are put with a good bit of fresh butter into a casserole on the fire, allowed to half-cook in this way, after which the sorrel and little peas are added. When all has been cooked and reduced, the vegetables are moistened with good consommé that was prepared expressly with good meat and fowl; the whole was boiled for a half-hour, then removed from the fire to cool, and put into bottles, closed, etc., so as to give the julienne a half-hour's boiling in the water-bath, etc.; it was preserved for more than two years. The julienne without meat is made in the same way, except that instead of consommé, the vegetables are wet, when they are properly cooked, with a clear purée, that may be made from kidney beans, lentils, or from large green peas, that have been preserved, and it is given likewise a half-hour's boiling in the water-bath, etc.

CULLIS FROM ROOTS.

I have composed and prepared a cullis from roots by the ordinary processes. It was so dark that soup for a dozen persons could be made from a liter, by adding two liters of water to it before heating as for ordinary use. When cooled, it was put into bottles so as to give it a half-hour's boiling in the water-bath, etc.

TOMATOES OR LOVE APPLES.

The tomatoes are gathered well matured, when they have acquired their fine color. After they have been washed and drained, they are cut into pieces and put to soften in a well tinned copper vessel. When they have been softened and reduced a third of their volume, they were strained through a sieve, sufficiently fine to retain the seeds; the whole strained, the decoction was replaced on the stove, and concentrated so that there remained only a third of its total volume; after cooling in stoneware dishes, it was put directly into bottles, etc., so as to give it a good boiling only in the water-bath, etc.

I have not yet made experiments upon flowers, but there is no doubt that this new method will give valuable and economical results.

MEDICINAL AND POT-HERBS.

I have filled a bottle with peppermint in leaf and in full flower, and pressed it down with a truncheon so as to make it hold more, properly closed, etc., so as to give a short boiling in the water-bath, etc. It is preserved perfectly. One could operate in like manner on all the

plants which one wished to preserve in
leaf. The preserver will have to calculate the degree of heat which is suitable
to give to each of these on which he will
work. (1.)

---

(1) The method of extracting the juice of the
plants by water has more or less objection; all
of those, the principle of which is very fugitive
and easily evaporated, lose excessively, even in
lukewarm water, and much more, when the
water is raised to a higher degree of heat and
when the plants are left a long time to digest.
The aromatic plants are infused, when it is
desired to preserve the aroma, and not to charge
the water with the extractive principle which
the plant contains. In this way tea and coffee
are made by infusion; all the theories, ancient
and modern, and all the new apparatus conceived for holding the aroma of coffee, also leave
much to be desired.

Boiling which is often employed for extracting the aroma from plants by means of distilla-
tion, notwithstanding that all the apparatus
used is closed, denatures the products oftenest.
Not only the principles extracted by the water
which are already lost through this primary
operation, but there is scarcely any of the prop-

JUICES OF HERBS.

I have preserved very well the juices of plants, such as those of lettuce, chervil, borage, wild chicory, watercress, etc. They were prepared and cleansed by the ordinary processes, closed, etc., so as to boil them in the water-bath, etc.

FRUITS AND THEIR JUICES.

Fruits and their juices demand the greatest celerity in the preparatory processes, and particularly in the application of the heat in the water-bath.

---

erty remaining after the evaporation to which they have been subjected to form the extracts. The extracts can therefore represent only the semblance of the soluble and nutritive properties of the vegetable and animal substances, since the heat necessary for forming the extract by means of evaporation, destroyed the aroma and nearly all of the properties which the substance contained.

It is not necessary to await perfect maturity of fruits to preserve them whole or in quarters, because they soften in the water-bath; it is also not best to take those at the beginning of the season, nor those at the end. The first and the last are never of as good quality or perfume as those which are gathered in the proper season, which is when the major part of the harvest is found in maturity.

RED AND WHITE CURRANTS IN CLUSTERS.

I have gathered the red and white currants separately, not too ripe; I select the best, and the finest and most suitable clusters; put them in bottles with care to heap them lightly when on the bench, so as to fill the spaces; after which they are closed, etc., put in the water-bath, and given careful attention so that as soon as it starts in ebullition or to boil, it is removed quickly from the stove, and a quarter of an hour after, the water is let out of the bater-bath through the valve, etc.

RED AND WHITE CURRANTS PICKED.

The red and white currants are picked separately, put in bottles and completed like those in clusters, with equal care in the water-bath. I preserve many more of the picked, because the clusters always give a harshness to the juice.

CHERRIES, RASPBERRIES, MULBERRIES, and BLACK CURRANTS.

These fruits are gathered not too ripe, so that they may crush less in the operation. They are put separately into bottles and heaped lightly when on the bench, closed, etc., and finished like, and with equal care as, currants.

JUICE OF RED CURRANTS.

The red currants are gathered well ripened, crushed upon a fine sieve, and the marc which remains on the sieve put in the press so as to extract all the juice that may remain, which is mixed with the first. The whole is perfumed with a little strawberry juice. The decoction is then passed through a finer sieve than the first, put in bottles, etc., and then in the water-bath, giving the same attention as for currants, etc.

I work in the same way with the juice of white currants, and thorny barberries, as well as with those of pomegranate, oranges, lemons, etc.

STRAWBERRIES.

I have made many different kinds of experiments upon the strawberry without being able to obtain its perfume; it has been necessary to have recourse to sugar. Consequently I have crushed and strained the strawberries on the sieve as in making jellies, for a pound of strawberries, a half pound of powdered sugar is added with the juice of half a lemon, the whole well mixed, and the

decoction put into bottles, closed, etc.,
left in the water-bath until ebullition
started, etc. This method has succeeded
very well, except that much of the color
was lost, but that deficiency can be sup-
plied.

APRICOTS.

For the table, the common apricot and
the apricot peach, the two most thriv-
ing, are the best kinds for preserving.
Those on the espalier do not have nearly so much flavor and aroma. Ordinarily I mix enough of the two kinds together, inasmuch as the first sustains the
other which has more juice and which
softens more through the action of the
heat; however, one can prepare them
separately, if the precaution be taken to
give a few minutes less in the water-
bath to the apricot peach; that is to say,
it is necessary to remove it from the
stove as soon as the water-bath com-
mences to boil, whereas for the other, it
is not removed from the fire until after
the water-bath is at the first boiling.

The apricots are gathered when ripe, but slightly firm, that is when by pressing lightly between the fingers, the stone is detached. As soon as gathered, I cut them in halves lengthwise, remove the stone, and the thinnest skin possible. According to the opening of the vessels, if they be in halves or in quarters, I put them in bottles, tap them on the bench so as to fill the spaces; to each bottle is added 12 to 15 of the almonds from the stones which have been broken; they are closed, etc., and put in the water-bath to give only a boiling, and immediately removed from the stove with the same precaution employed with regard to the currants, etc.

PEACHES.

The large *Mignonne* and the *Calande* are the two kinds of peaches in which are united the best quality and aroma; in default of these two kinds, the best possible are taken for preserving by the same processes as those employed for apricots.

NECTARINES.

The nectarine is taken well-ripened, that is to say, riper than the peach, inasmuch as it holds up better under the action of the heat, and besides the skin is left on in preserving. As to the rest, I operate in the same manner as for apricots and peaches, and always look after the water-bath, as for currants.

GREENGAGES AND MIRABELLE PLUMS.

I have used the greengages whole, as well as the other large plums, with stem and nut, and even the Perdrigons, and the Alberges, which have succeeded very well with me; but the objection is that very few of these large plums are contained in a large vessel since in heaping them up, one cannot fill the spaces, at least without totally crushing them, and after they have been subjected to the action of the heat in the water-bath, they are reduced so that the vessels are half empty. Consequently I have given up this method as too expensive and have preserved the large plums only after cutting them in halves and removing the stone. This method is easier and more economical; the stoppers of the size to close the large vessels were much dearer and the very fine cork scarcer; on the other hand, the vessels of small or average opening are much easier to close properly and in consequence the operation is more certain. As to the Mirabelle and all other small plums, they are prepared whole with the stones, after having removed the stem, because they are more easily heaped up, and leave only very small spaces in the vessels. For all plums, whole or cut in halves, generally the same processes are employed, with the same care and attention as for the apricot and the peach.

PEARS OF ALL KINDS.

When the pears are peeled, cut in quarters, and cleaned of their seeds, as

well as the cores, they are put in bottles,
etc., for to put in the water-bath. The
degree of heat is watched carefully, so
that they should only come to ebullition,
when they are arranged with a knife.
To cook the pears they are given 5 or 6
minutes boiling in the water-bath. For
the fallen pears it is necessary to give a
quarter-hour's boiling, etc.

CHESTNUTS.

The head of the chestnut is pricked
with the point of a knife as for parching
them. They are put in bottles, etc., so
as to give them a boiling in the water-
bath, etc.

TRUFFLES.

After having properly washed and
brushed the truffles to remove all the
earth, the surface is taken off lightly
with a knife. Afterward, according to
the diameter or the opening of the mouth
of the vessels, they are put in bottles,

whole or cut in pieces; the residue is put in separate bottles; all properly closed, etc. They are put in the water-bath to receive an hour's boiling, etc. (It is not necessary to enjoin that the truffles should be wholesome and recently gathered.)

MUSHROOMS.

Mushrooms are taken, coming out of the bed well formed and fairly firm. After having picked and washed them, they are put in a casserole on the stove with a bit of butter or some good olive oil so as to draw out the water. They are left on the stove until this water is reducd to half; removed to let them cool in an earthen pan, then they are put in bottles so as to give a good boiling in the water-bath, etc.

GRAPE MUST OR SWEET WINE.

In 1808, during the vintage, I have taken the black grape, gathered from the vine with care; after having removed the green and rotten ones, they are picked from the stem, afterward crushed on a fine sieve. The marc which remained on the sieve is put under the press, so as to extract any juice which might remain in it. The two products, that from the press and that from the sieve, are put together into a small cask. After having left it to settle for twenty-four hours, it is put into bottles, etc., so as to give it a good boiling in the water-bath, etc. (1.) When the operation is completed, the bottles are removed from the boiler; the action of the heat had precipitated a little color that the must had acquired in the preparation, and the must had become very clear. It was arranged on laths in my laboratory as one places wine.

I have repeated all these experiments the 10th of September, 1809, in the pres-

---

(1) I have put the residues from the puncheon with the marc from the press into the vintage.

ence of the special commission named by His Excellency, the Minister of the Interior, and composed of persons of the highest attainment in the art.

Some newly started experiments as well as many others that I propose to try upon various substances will be described in a work that I expect to publish as soon as I shall be able to report on their result.

Manner of making use of the prepared and preserved substances.

MEATS, GAME, FOWL, FISH.

An ordinary *pot-au-feu* of which the degree of cooking has been calculated in the preparation as well as the application of the heat in the water-bath, need not be heated to the degree needed to obtain soup and boiled meat.

For greater economy, and less multiplication of vessels, a good consommé, such as indicated, is more desirable, since the beef, as well as the consommé, only needs to be heated, and an average of one-half or two-thirds of the water which is added to the consommé is obtained as a good soup.

Likewise a liter bottle of consommé, by means of two liters of water which you add to it at the moment of using, gives twelve portions of soup by adding to it a little salt. In this way one could have at home, at little expense, a small supply for use during warm weather when it is so difficult to be procured, particularly in the country.

All the meats, fowl, game, fish, etc., which have received three-quarters cooking in preparation and the remainder in the water-bath, as indicated, on taking from the vessel need only be heated to the proper degree for serving them on the table. If it happens, for example, that on taking a substance from a vessel, it is not sufficiently cooked, through failure of the preparatory processes or through not receiving sufficient heat in the water-bath, in that case it requires only putting it on the stove to give it the necessary cooking. In consequence, when the worker has taken proper care that his preparations are seasoned and cooked properly, they may be readily and conveniently used in all cases, inasmuch as on the one side one need only to heat them, and on the other side, at a pinch, they could be eaten cold.

The substances prepared and preserved in this manner do not require, as one might think, to be eaten as soon as they are opened. The food from the same vessel may be eaten for 8 or 10 days after it has been opened (1), provided only that the stopper be replaced immediately after one has taken the required amount; so that the capacity of

---

(1) See the report made to the Society for the Encouragement of National Industry, by M. Bouriat, in the name of the commission. Two half-liter bottles, one of milk, the other of whey, opened after twenty to thirty days, had been reclosed with little care, yet these two substances had preserved all their properties.

the vessel could be regulated from one to 25 liters and more according to the amount of the presumed consumption.

MEAT AND FOWL JELLY.

A jelly well prepared and preserved, removed carefully in small portions from the vessel, can be used to garnish cold meats, or it may be softened easily in the vessel in the water-bath, after opening it; afterwards it can be melted on a plate so as to reset it as a glaze before serving.

In a number of emergencies a cook lacks the necessary substances to make sauces, etc., but with the essence of meats, fowl, ham, etc., as well as with the foundation of glazes properly prepared and preserved, he can obtain them in a moment.

BROTH OR PECTORAL JELLY.

Regarding pectoral jelly, prepared and preserved as indicated, the use made of it may be, on taking from the bottle, the diluting of it with more or less boiling water, or using it cold, in the proportions deemed by the chefs most suitable in the various cases.

MILK AND CREAM.

Cream, milk, and whey, prepared and preserved as indicated, are used in the same way as the fresh in daily use.

Since cream and milk are preserved perfectly in this manner, there is no doubt but that one could even preserve the creamed side dishes, as well as those for ices which, since they had been prepared and finished before being put in bottles, need only to be heated slightly in the water-bath, after having been opened, so as to facilitate removal from the vessel. One could thus procure creams and ices in succession and at a moment's notice.

VEGETABLES.

The vegetables put in bottles without

being cooked and subjected afterward
to the action of the water-bath in the
manner indicated need to be prepared
on taking from the vessel so as to use
them. This preparation may be according to the taste and the desires of each
one and may conform to the different
methods employed in season. It is necessary to give attention to washing the
vegetables on taking out of the vessel,
and likewise so as to facilitate their removal the bottle is filled with lukewarm
water, and after draining it of this first
water, the vegetables are washed in a
second water a little warmer, and after
this draining they are prepared with or
without meat.

WHITE KIDNEY BEANS.

As in season, the white kidney beans
are blanched in water with a little salt
on removal from the bottle. When
properly cooked, they are removed from
the stove, and left in this cooking water
a half hour and even an hour, so as to

make them tenderer, afterwards they
are prepared with or without meat.

FRENCH BEANS.

In the same way the French beans
are blanched when they have not been
cooked sufficiently by the preserving
processes, which happens sometimes, as
well as with artichokes, asparagus, cauliflower, etc. If they are sufficiently
cooked on taking from the vessel, they
are only washed with hot water, so as
to prepare them afterwards.

SMALL GREEN PEAS

The small green peas are prepared in
much the same manner. If in season
they are found poorly prepared, it is
the cook who receives the blame; but in
the winter if they are found poor, great
care is taken to put the blame on the one
who has preserved them, though poor
preparations are to be attributed oftenest to bad butter or oil, or to rancid fat

which was used without care or through
economy; sometimes they are prepared
two hours too soon, or left to deteriorate
and to stick to the bottom of the casserole on the stove, with the result that the
butter is turned to oil and tastes like
burned sugar, or they are prepared without care and in too great haste; it is in
this way that one is served with the peas
that are swimming in water; but every
one to his own way.   Here is mine.

As soon as the small peas are washed
and well drained (it is not necessary to
leave this vegetable in water, any more
than the broad beans, as it detracts from
its quality), I put them with a bit of
good fresh butter in a casserole on the
stove and add a bouquet of parsley and
green onions; after having sautéd them
for some time in the butter, I sprinkle
them with a little starch, just to flour the
peas, and wet them an instant later with
boiling water; they are boiled for a full
quarter-hour, until the sauce is reduced;
then seasoned with salt and a little pepper, and left on the stove to reduce

further, when they are removed from
the fire so as to add, for a bottle of small
peas, fresh butter as large as a walnut,
and a tablespoon of powdered sugar.
They are allowed to stew well until the
butter is melted, without returning to
the stove, and then set in a heap on a
plate that has been heated. I have often
observed that in adding the sugar to the
little peas when they are on the stove,
and giving them only a boiling, the peas
are shrivelled and the sauce thinned so
that it cannot be thickened; thus one
must take great care not to put the sugar
and the last butter with the peas until
the moment of serving them, and after
they have been withdrawn from the
stove. It is the only way to finish them
properly, because the butter should
never appear in the sauce of little peas,
no more in summer than in winter.
There is still another way of preparing
the little peas, and which should agree
with many persons; it consists in cooking them in water only; when they are
cooked, the water is drained off so as

to stew them with a piece of good fresh butter, salt, pepper, and sugar, all together on a gentle fire, then to serve them at once on a very hot dish. It is necessary to take care that the little peas should not cook with the seasoning, otherwise the butter will become oily, and the sugar soften the peas so they dissolve in the water.

BROAD BEANS.

The small broad beans are prepared, shelled as well as unshelled, by the same process and with the same care used with little peas.

The large preserved peas make excellent purée; they are equally good with meat. As regards asparagus, artichokes, cauliflower, etc., they are prepared ordinarily after having been washed, etc. Peas, beans, kidney beans, and all kinds of vegetables, may be three-quarters cooked, seasoning them at the time when they are to be used without further preparation on opening, putting them in

bottles or other vessels, when cooled,
closing them, etc., and giving them a
half-hour's boiling in the water-bath; by
this means the vegetables may be well-
preserved, and all prepared, so that one
could make use of them at the instant,
without other attention than that of
heating; and further it is true that in this
case the vegetables could be eaten cold;
one may avoid in this way all embarrass-
ment on voyages by land and sea, etc.

CHICORY AND SPINACH.

I prepare chicory and spinach in the
customary way, either with or without
meat; each half-liter bottle contains two
or three dishes, according to their size.
When only a single dish is needed, the
bottle is closed, and kept for another
day.

JULIENNE.

After having emptied a liter bottle of
preserved julienne, I add two liters of
boiling water with a little salt, and I

have a soup for a dozen to fifteen persons.

CULLIS OF ROOTS.

Like the julienne, cullis of roots, purées of lentils, carrots, onions, etc., well prepared, furnish excellent soups in a moment with the greatest economy.

All the meals, such as oatmeal, rice, barley, semolina, vermicelli, and generally all the nourishing and easily digested pastes, should be seasoned and prepared, either with or without meat, even with milk, before being subjected to the preserving processes, so as to facilitate their use at sea or to the armies at the time of need.

TOMATOES.

I use preserved tomatoes or love apples, for the same purpose as in season; on removal from the bottle they need only to be heated and properly seasoned.

SORREL.

As the sorrel preserved by the same processes indicated differs in no way from that in the month of June, on removing from the vessel, it is used in the same manner as in season.

MINT.

As for peppermint and all the plants which can be preserved in branches by the same processes, they may be used in the same manner as herb essences.

FRUITS.

· The manner of using fruits preserved by the processes indicated, consists, 1st, to put each fruit as it is found in the bottle, in a compotier, without adding sugar to it, because many persons,.particularly women, prefer the fruits with their natural juice; these compotes are accompanied by another compotier of syrup of grapes or of powdered sugar for those who like them. I have discovered from experiments that the syrup of

grapes preserves the aroma and the
acidity of fruits infinitely better than
sugar. This is the simplest and most
economical style of preparing excellent
compotes, a style so much the more convenient since each one can satisfy his
taste for more or less sugar. 2nd, to
make sweet compotes, a pound of preserved fruit is taken, the kind is immaterial, which, on taking from the bottle
with its juice, is put in a sauce-pan
on the stove with four ounces of grape
syrup. As soon as it begins to boil, it
is taken from the stove, and the scum
removed by means of a piece of
crumpled paper that is applied to the
surface. As soon as it is skimmed, the
fruit is taken carefully from the syrup
so as to put it in a compotier. After
having reduced the syrup on the stove
to half its volume, it is poured on the
fruit. The fruits prepared in this way
are sufficiently sweet, and also as savory
as a fresh compote made in season.

COMPOTES WITH BRANDY.

3rd. For the compotes made with brandy, which may be of cherries, apricots, greengages, pears, peaches, Mirabelle plums, etc., a pound of fruit with juice, which is taken indiscriminately, is put in a sauce-pan on the stove with a quarter-pound of grape syrup. When about to boil, it is skimmed, after which the fruit is taken carefully out of the syrup and put in a vessel; the syrup is left on the stove until it is reduced a quarter of its volume; afterwards it is taken from the stove, so as to add to it a glass of good brandy; and, after having been well stirred, the hot syrup is poured over the fruit in the vessel, which is carefully closed, so that the fruit is penetrated better by the syrup, etc.

One may do likewise with the preserved pear and peach of the cooked compotes, as well as compotes with Burgundy wine, with cinnamon, etc.

MARMALADES.

4th. I make marmalade from apricots, peaches, greengages, and Mirabelle plums by the following process. For a pound of preserved fruit, a half pound of grape syrup is used. They are cooked over a strong fire, and carefully stirred with a spatula so as to avoid burning the fruit; when the marmalade is cooked to a light consistence, it is removed, because the preserves cooked the least are always the best. As the preserved fruits give one the facility for making preserves in proportion only to one's needs, in cooking them lightly, one can always have excellent fresh preserves.

CURRANT JELLY.

The way to make currant jelly with the juice of preserved fruit is very simple; a half pound of sugar is used for a pound of currant juice (which should be flavored with a little strawberry). After having clarified and cooked the sugar to the break, the currant is put in, and is given three or four boilings; when it falls from the skimmer in small sheets no larger than a lentil, it is taken from the stove to put it in jars, etc.

CURRANT SYRUP.

To make currant syrup the juice is heated close to boiling, and removed to strain it. By this means it is obtained clear and deprived of the mucilage. As soon as it is strained, a half pound of grape syrup is added for each pound of fruit, the whole put on the stove. When it is cooked to the consistence of a light syrup, it is taken off the stove so as to put it in bottles when it is cooled.

There is a simpler and more economical way to make use, not only of currant juice but of those of all fruits from which acid beverages may be made. This consists simply in putting a tablespoon of the juice of currant or any other bottled preserve into a glass of water slightly sweetened with grape syrup. This is easy to have at all times in one's own home or to procure at little expense some of these juices thus preserved; it is in this way that for fifteen years we serve currant juice at home, and oftener we prepare this lemonade without sugar or syrup.

ICES.

I have prepared and made ices from currants, raspberries, apricots, and peaches, as well as from strawberries, preserved as indicated, by the method employed in the season for these fruits.

I have made these experiments to forestall any further question of grape syrup, maintaining that this product, the slightly sour or acid grape syrup, brought to perfection at the manufactory of M. Privat, at Meze, will replace, shortly and with advantage, cane sugar in the preparation of fruit ices.

As I have already observed, the grape syrup preserves the aroma of all fruits better than cane sugar. The sugar masks the taste of the fruits to such an extent that one is obliged to add some lemon juice to all fruit ices, so as to again restore the aroma; but if the slightly sour grape syrup be used, one can dispense with lemons and the fruit ices are much mellower. The sweet grape syrup may be used with success with all the cream ices.

LIQUEURS.

I have made liqueurs and ratafias with the juices of preserved fruits and sweetened with grape syrup. These preparations yield nothing to the best household liqueurs.

The simple and easy means that I indicate for preparing all the preserved fruits for daily use prove conclusively that this method, as certain as it is useful, will occasion the greatest economy in the consumption of cane sugar. The consumers, and the chefs particularly, who through circumstances are obliged during the summer to start with a considerable stock of it for syrups, preserves, and liqueurs, as well as for pharmaceutical articles, through this foreign commodity may dispense with it; in short it will suffice for them to provide their stock of fruits during the harvest, and to preserve them by this new method, so as to provide sugar only in proportion to their needs. It will result in that the major portion of all the fruits thus preserved will be consumed without, or with very little sugar; that a great deal will be prepared with grape syrup, and that only for indispensable articles, and for satisfying habitual consumers, as well as a luxury for some tables, that the cane sugar will be employed.

It will follow from this that in a good year it will not be necessary to provide a stock of sugar for the time of scarcity, and that one will obtain with little expense the same pleasure with fruits preserved for two, three, and four years, as in the years of abundance.

CHESTNUTS.

On taking the preserved chestnuts from the vessel they are plunged into fresh water, powdered with a little fine salt, and roasted in the frying pan over a bright fire. In this way, they are excellent; one may dispense with the wetting, but it is always necessary that they be roasted over a bright fire.

The preserved truffles are employed in the same way and for the same purposes, as when they have been freshly gathered, and also mushrooms.

GRAPE MUST.

When I made my first experiments on preserving grape must in its fresh state, *instruction upon the means of making up the deficiency of sugar in the principal things, in which use is made*

*of it in medicine and in domestic eco-
nomy by M. Parmentier* was not yet
known to me. It is from this valuable
source that I have obtained methods for
employing in my new experiments two
hundred bottles of grape must that I had
preserved six months before.

1st. I have made very fine grape
syrup by following the processes of M.
Parmentier, which I give literally.

PREPARATION OF GRAPE SYRUP.

"Twenty-four pints of must are taken
and half of it put in a large kettle on the
stove, with care to avoid too strong
ebullition. New liquor is added in proportion to the amount evaporated as it is
skimmed and stirred to increase evaporation. When the whole of the must is
added, the liquid is skimmed and taken
from the stove, and there is added to it
either washed ashes, enclosed in a little
bag, whiting, or chalk reduced to
powder and diluted previously with a
little must, until there is no longer effer-

vescence, or a kind of bubbling in the liquor, which should be stirred. By this means the acid contained in the grapes is separated or neutralized; one is assured that the liquor has no more acid when the blue paper which is dipped in it is not colored red. Then the kettle is replaced on the stove, after having had two beaten eggs put in it and left an instant to settle. The liquor is filtered through woolen cloth fastened to a wooden frame, twelve to fifteen inches square, in a manner ito occupy little room; it is boiled anew to continue the evaporation.

So as to know if the syrup be cooked, it is let fall from a spoon on a plate; if the drop falls without breaking and spreading out, or if in separating in two the parts only draw near lengthwise, then one judges that it has the required consistence.

It is poured into an unglazed earthenware vessel, and after it has cooled perfectly, is distributed into bottles of aver-

age capacity, cleaned, dried, properly
corked, and carried to the cellar. It is
necessary that a bottle once opened
should have the neck reversed each time
that one is served from it, and that it
should not remain a long time without
emptying.

It is hardly possible to determine pre-
cisely the quantity of chalk or ashes that
it is necessary to employ, it is less necessary in the south than in the north, but
in any case, the excess should not cause
injury, since it remains on the filter
mixed with the other insoluble salts and
the scum.

If in view of preserving these syrups
for a longer time, the cooking is carried
too far, one may be deceived because it
will not be long in crystallizing in the
bottom of the bottles and not be thin;
on the contrary, if it is not evaporated
sufficiently, it will ferment soon; a
thrifty housekeeper will not make these
syrups twice without understanding the
degree of cooking necessary to give

them, better than one could indicate to her, the point at which it is advisable that it should be arrested."

It is with this same syrup that I have prepared compotes, preserves, syrups, and acid beverages, as well as liqueurs and ratafias from all the fruits of which I have spoken.

2d. I have made syrup with the same must and by the same processes, except that I have only cooked the ratafia lightly, that is to say, a fourth or less than the syrup, desiring to be assured if by means of the application of the heat of the water-bath by the indicated processes it would be preserved. The syrup, when cooled, I have put into three half liter bottles, one full and the two others having a space of a quarter and a half; I have closed, tied, etc., and subjected them in the water-bath to boiling only, etc. I have not noticed any difference in the full bottle from those partly empty, and all three are preserved perfectly.

3d. I have taken six pints of preserved grape must to which has been added two pints of good old brandy, of twenty-two degrees, with two pounds of grape syrup that I had prepared. This preparation, mixed well, has served to make four different liqueurs by means of infusions of apricot stones, mint, orange flower, and anise seed that had been prepared in advance; these liqueurs, well filtered, have been found very good and sweet enough.

4th. I have taken two bottles of preserved must, opened, and transferred the must to two other clean bottles, that have been immediately closed and tied; these two bottles were left upright for ten days; after this interval, the liqueur blew the cork out like the best champagne, and effervesced similarly.

5th. I have repeated this last experiment in the same manner. After twelve to fifteen days, not noting any appearance of fermentation in the bottles, I opened them so as to restore air to them, and put a tablespoonful of raspberry juice into two of them. After having reclosed and tied them, they were left upright again for eight days; at the end of this time, the white and the red had blown out the cork; they effervesced perfectly and were of very agreeable taste, particularly the red, flavored with the raspberries.

After the experiments made with the Massy grape, it is more than probable that in the south as well as in good vineyards, one may obtain infinitely valuable results by making use of this method. One may preserve grape must for sweet syrup in this manner by concentrating at will to the consistence of syrup after having deacidified it for sweet syrup; or if these syrups are concentrated on the stove, to 25, 30, or 33 by aerometer, which degree is immaterial, they may be preserved for many years by submitting them to heat in the water-bath according to the preparatory processes that I have employed.

By means of these processes, easy to put in practice, and above all of slight expense in execution, one may obtain syrups clearer, whiter (they might be made of black grapes), and of a frank and free sweetness, devoid of the taste of molasses and of caramel; this, one has not yet been able to avoid in grape syrup when it is desired to give a degree of cooking suitable for keeping.

It is in this manner that, preserved in bottles or demijohns of any capacity, this valuable product can be exported to long distances, in all seasons, and come from Bergerac, from Meze, and from all the manufactories of the South, improving the products of our small vineyards, and permitting all classes of society to enjoy this useful resource.

From the statement of all the experiments, given in detail, it is seen that this new method of preservation is founded on a unique principle, the application of

heat of suitable degree to various substances after having deprived them as
far as possible from contact with air (1).
It is not in question here, as in the experiments of the chemists of Bordeaux,
the destruction of the mass of foods,
having on one side the animal jelly and
on the other the fiber deprived of all its
juice and resembling cooked leather. It
is not the question, as with bouillon tablets, of preparing at great expense a

---

(1) At the first glance one might believe that
a substance, either raw or prepared on the stove,
afterwards put in bottles, after having been
vacuumized, and closed perfectly, would be preserved similarly without the application of the
heat of the water-bath. This would be a mistake because all the attempts that I have made,
have demonstrated that the two essential factors,
the absolute deprivation from contact with the
exterior air (that which is found in the interior
need not cause anxiety, because it has been rendered harmless by the action of the heat) and
application of the heat in the water-bath are
indispensable to each other for the perfect preservation of foods.

tenacious paste more adapted to de-
range the stomach than to furnish a
healthful food.

The problem consists in preserving all
nutritive substances with their characteristic and constituent properties. This
is a problem which I have solved, as has
been demonstrated by my experiments.
(1).

---

(1) Some distinguished men, but perhaps too
bookish in their spirit of system and of preju-
dice, have declared against my method, alleging
a pretended impossibility.

Yet, according to the principles of sound phil-
osophy is it then so difficult to produce proof
for the cause of the preservation of foods by
my process? Cannot one see that the application of heat in the water-bath should slowly
work a fusion of the constituent and ferment-
able principles, so that there is no longer any
agent there of the fermentation that dominated;
this predominance is an essential condition in
order that the fermentation take place at least
with a certain promptitude. The air, without
which there is no fermentation, being excluded,

It is to the solution of this problem that I have given twenty years of work

---

there are two essential causes which can render proof of the success of my method, the theory of which naturally appears the result from the means put in practise.

In short, if one brings together all the known methods, all the experiments and the observations which have been made in ancient and modern times upon the means of preserving foods, one will everywhere recognize the heat as the principal agent that directs, it may be hardening, it may be the preservation of vegetable and animal products.

Fabroni has proved that heat applied to grape must destroys the ferment of this *vegeto-animal,* which is pre-eminently the leaven. Thenard has made similar experiments upon currants, cherries, and other fruits. The heat experiments of Vilaris and of M. Cazales, learned chemists of Bordeaux, which have been made in desiccating meats by means of stoves, proved likewise that the application of heat destroys the agents of putrefaction.

Desiccation, boiling, evaporation, as well as

and thought as well as my fortune.
Blessed already in being able to serve
my fellow-citizens and humanity I rely
on the justice, generosity, and intelligence of a wise government, that never
ceases to encourage and protect all useful discoveries. It will be seen that
the author of this method of preservation will not be able to obtain from
the discovery even recompense for his
pains and expenses. The greatest importance, in short, of this process, its
principal use is for the needs of
civil and military hospitals, and particularly for those of the navy. It is in
these administrations that I can find
employment for my methods in a manner useful to the state, as well as the
just reward for my labor. I await the
gracious inspection of the Ministry, and
my hopes will not be deceived.

---

caustic or savory substances that are employed
for the preservation of alimentary products
serve to prove that the heat produces similar
effects, etc.

GENERAL OBSERVATIONS.

The bottles and other vessels of any capacity, suitable for the preservation of foods, require only a small number to be made at one time. One can always use them anew, provided they be rinsed as soon as emptied. Good cork, twine, and wire, are not a large expense. As soon as this method becomes known, one will find suitable bottles and vessels at crockery-ware dealers, corks of all sizes and squeezed in the vise will be furnished by the cork-cutters, as well as the prepared wire. It is always prudent to procure the corks before the bottles so as to supply oneself with those that have openings proportionate to the size of the stoppers that one has; because it may happen, as I have found often, that one may not be able to find corks of the desired sizes.

The glass-works of Garre, of Seves, and of Premontres near Coucy-le-Chateau, are already manufacturing bottles

and jars necessary to the method of
preservation. The last, which has furnished them to me for four years, is the
one with which I am best satisfied. The
means of properly closing depends on a
little practise only; to close a dozen bottles with confidence and precision will
suffice to familiarize one with the manner, more particularly with the glass.
Everywhere and every day, wines, liqueurs, etc., are put in bottles to voyage
by land and sea to the most distant
regions; even glass demijohns of forty
and eighty liters capacity, full of oil of
vitriol and other liquids, have made voyages. It will be the same with all animal and vegetable products preserved
in bottles or other glass vessels when
one acquires the habit of using the necessary care and precautions. It is what
one needs most. How much valuable
liqueurs and other valuable substances
should be better preserved and which
are often lost or altered for the want of
having been properly corked!

No one will doubt after all the ex-

periments which I give in detail that
the putting in practise of this new method which, as one can judge for himself,
unites to the greatest economy a degree
of perfection hitherto unhoped for, and
which procures the following advantages:

1st. That of considerably diminishing the consumption of cane sugar and
of extending to the greatest extent the
manufacture of grape syrup.

2d. That of preserving for use
everywhere and in all seasons, food products, of medicaments, of which there
will be occasions of great abundance in
certain seasons or in various countries;
substances which are wasted or sold at
low price, whereas in other circumstances
they double and quadruple in value, and
it is even impossible to get them at any
price; such are, among others, butter
and eggs.

3d. That of procuring for the civil
and military hospitals, likewise for the

army, the most valuable assistance of which the details are unnecessary. But the greatest advantage of this method consists particularly in its application to the uses of the navy; for long voyages it will furnish fresh and wholesome nourishment on board the vessels of His Majesty, with a saving of more than fifty per cent. The sailors, in their illness, will have broth and various acid beverages, vegetables, fruits, in a word, they will be able to enjoy a multitude of foods and medicaments which alone will often suffice to prevent or to cure the diseases which are contracted at sea, and principally and most dreaded of all, scurvy. These advantages are well worthy of fixing the attention, when one reflects that the salted provisions, and above all their poor quality, have done more to destroy men than shipwreck and the fury of combat.

4th. The physician will find in this method the means of relieving humanity, by the readiness in finding everywhere, and in all seasons, the animal substances and all the vegetables as well as their juices, preserved with all their qualities and natural virtues; through the same means he will obtain infinitely valuable assistance in the products of remote regions preserved in all their freshness.

5th. From this method a new branch of industry will result relative to the productions of France, through the exportation and importation into the interior and to foreign parts, of the commodities of which nature has favored the different countries.

6th. This method will facilitate the exportation of the wines from many vineyards. In fact, the wines which are scarcely able to hold up for a year, and, yet without changing, may be sent to foreign lands and be preserved many years.

In short, one such invention ought to enrich the domain of chemistry, and should become a general benefit to all nations that derive from it the most valuable results.

So many benefits and an infinity of others, which present themselves to the imagination of the reader, produced by one and the same cause only, are a source of wonder.

END.

TABLE OF CONTENTS.

(113)

END OF THE TABLE.

Printed in Great Britain
by Amazon